WRITER'S
TOOLBOX

JUST THE FACTS
Writing Your Own Research Report

by Nancy Loewen   illustrated by Dawn Beacon

Picture Window Books
Minneapolis, Minnesota

Editor: Jill Kalz
Designer: Nathan Gassman
Page Production: Melissa Kes
Editorial Director: Nick Healy
Creative Director: Joe Ewest
The illustrations in this book were created with acrylics.

Picture Window Books
151 Good Counsel Drive
P.O. Box 669
Mankato, MN 56002-0669
877-845-8392
www.picturewindowbooks.com

Library of Congress Cataloging-in-Publication Data
Loewen, Nancy, 1964–
Just the facts : writing your own research report /
by Nancy Loewen ; illustrated by Dawn Beacon.
p. cm. — (Writer's toolbox)
Includes index.
ISBN 978-1-4048-5519-9 (library binding)
ISBN 978-1-4048-5702-5 (paperback)
1. Report writing—Juvenile literature. I. Beacon, Dawn, ill.
II. Title.
LB1047.3.L64 2009
372.13028'1—dc22   2009006882

Special thanks to our adviser, Terry Flaherty, Ph.D., Professor of English, Minnesota State University, Mankato, for his expertise.

A research report is a special kind of writing assignment. You don't tell a story. You don't make things up. In fact, writing is one of the LAST steps in putting together a research report.

First you'll need to pick a topic. You'll learn what experts have to say about your topic. You'll take notes. You'll organize facts. And when you're done with those steps? THEN you'll write.

Writing a research report is a challenging task—but a fun one, too. By the time you've finished your report, you'll be a mini expert yourself!

polar bear—is losing its home because of global warming

vampire bat—drinks blood!

platypus—has a weird bill, lays eggs

koala—cute!

python—up to 33 feet long, and can swallow a goat!

~ Tool 1 ~

Every research report starts with a **TOPIC**. Pick one that interests you. The more interested you are, the more fun it will be. Make a list of possible ideas. Then start narrowing it down. Look up a few quick facts, if you're not sure about your choices.

~ Tool 2 ~

The research begins! Books, magazines, and newspapers are good **SOURCES** of information. So is the Internet. You might even talk to a person who is an expert on your topic.

If you use the Internet, make sure your sources are trustworthy. Look for well-known Web sites. If you're not sure, ask your teacher or librarian.

Try for at least three sources. If a book or article is too difficult (or too easy), put it aside and try to find something more fitting. Don't worry about your report the first time you read your sources. Just enjoy learning about your subject.

Where do platypuses live?

What do platypuses look like?

Do platypuses have any enemies?

What do platypuses eat?

~ Tool 3 ~

Once you're familiar with your topic, start **BRAINSTORMING.** Write down all the questions you might want to answer in your report. You probably won't be able to include everything in your report, but that's OK.

Do female platypuses really lay eggs?

How many eggs do they lay?

How long do platypuses live?

Are platypuses endangered?

What sounds do platypuses make?

How big is a platypus?

Do platypuses swim? Do they walk?

Are platypuses active in the day or night?

~ Tool 4 ~

The next step in writing a research report is to take **NOTES.** Index cards make note-taking easier. Write one of your brainstorming questions at the top of each card. As you re-read your sources, record the answers to your questions on the cards. You might need more than one card per question.

Include the name of your sources on your index cards, as well as page numbers or Web site addresses. If any questions come up later, you'll know exactly where to look.

Where do platypuses live?

Tasmania and Eastern Australia—_Platypus!_, page 10

beside streams, rivers, and lakes in eastern and southeastern Australia, stretching from Queensland down to Victoria and Tasmania—_A Platypus' World_, pages 3, 22

What do platypuses eat?

insects, larvae, shellfish, and worms—nationalgeographic.com

worms, insects, fish eggs, water plants, shrimp—
A Platypus' World, pages 3, 6

Introduction (riddle)

Where the platypus lives, how big it is

The snout

The tail

The feet

How the female lays eggs

Baby platypuses

Conclusion

~ Tool 5 ~

Writing your report will be easier if you plan ahead. An **OUTLINE** will help you do this. An outline lists the ideas of a report, in the order they will be presented.

Some outlines are very simple. The example here on the left is a simple outline. It lists general ideas rather than specific facts. Other outlines are detailed, like the one on the right. Use the type of outline that works best for you.

Introduction

riddle: What has a bill like a duck, a tail like a beaver, and feet like an otter?
- not a joke
- strange mammal but actually makes sense

habitat, appearance
- lives near lakes and streams in Australia and Tasmania
- about half the size of a cat
- brown, waterproof fur
- active mostly at night

snout
- dark rubbery skin, tiny holes with nerve endings
- nerves sense motion, help find food
- uses bill to dig up food
- eats worms, insects, shrimp, fish eggs

tail
- flat and wide, like a beaver's but is covered with fur
- uses tail and hind legs to steer while swimming
- uses tail to carry away dirt from digging

13

QUACK!

+

You've picked your topic. You've done your
research, taken notes, and made an outline.
It's time to write!

What has a bill like a duck, a tail like a beaver, and feet like
an otter? This question sounds like a joke. But it's not. The
answer is: a platypus! The platypus is one of the strangest
mammals on our planet. But when we take a close look, we
can see that this odd animal makes sense.

~ Tool 6 ~

The first paragraph in a research report is the **INTRODUCTION.** The introduction should do two things. It should get the reader's attention in some way. And it should state what the report will be about.

This introduction begins like a riddle. It "hooks" us. We know that the platypus is different from other mammals. And we want to keep reading, to find out why.

15

answer is: a platypus! The platypus is one of the strangest mammals on our planet. But when we take a close look, we can see that this odd animal makes sense.

Platypuses live near lakes and streams in eastern Australia and the island of Tasmania. They are about half the size of a cat. They have brown, waterproof fur. They are active mostly at night.

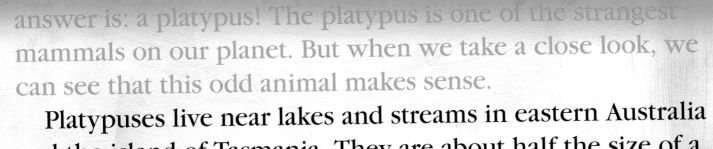

■ platypus habitat

Australia

Tasmania

~ Tool 7 ~

The **BODY** is the main part of a research report. It is usually three or more paragraphs. The body includes the most important information about the topic.

It's a good idea to provide some basic information early in your report. In this paragraph, we find out where platypuses live. We find out how big they are, too. If we didn't learn those things right away, we might wonder about them throughout the report.

17

cat. They have brown, waterproof fur. They are active mostly at night.

The most unusual part of a platypus is its bill, or snout. The bill is covered with dark rubbery skin. It has tiny holes all over it. Inside the holes are nerve endings. These nerves sense motion. They help the platypus find its food. Platypuses use their bills to dig up food from the mud. They eat shrimp, worms, fish eggs, and insects.

~ Tool 8 ~

The first sentence in a paragraph is called a **TOPIC SENTENCE.** It lets the reader know what will be talked about in that paragraph. It's like a mini introduction. After the topic sentence, every sentence that follows should add detail. Here the topic sentence introduces us to the platypus' bill.

is covered with dark rubbery skin. It has tiny holes all over it. Inside the holes are nerve endings. These nerves sense motion. They help the platypus find its food. Platypuses use their bills to dig up food from the mud. They eat shrimp, worms, fish eggs, and insects.

The platypus has a flat, wide tail. It's shaped like a beaver's tail. The tail is covered with fur. The platypus uses its tail and hind legs to steer while swimming. The platypus also uses its tail to carry away dirt when digging a burrow. Fat is stored in the tail, too. The fat gives the platypus extra energy during the winter months, when there is less food.

Like otters, platypuses have webbed feet. The platypus' front feet are like paddles. They help the platypus swim. On land, the webbing folds up between the platypus' claws. The platypus' short legs are on the side of its body. The platypus is a good swimmer, but a slow walker.

As you write your report, remember what you promised your reader in the introduction. Do your best to stay on track.

So far we have learned how the platypus uses its strange tail, feet, and bill. We see that the platypus does indeed make sense.

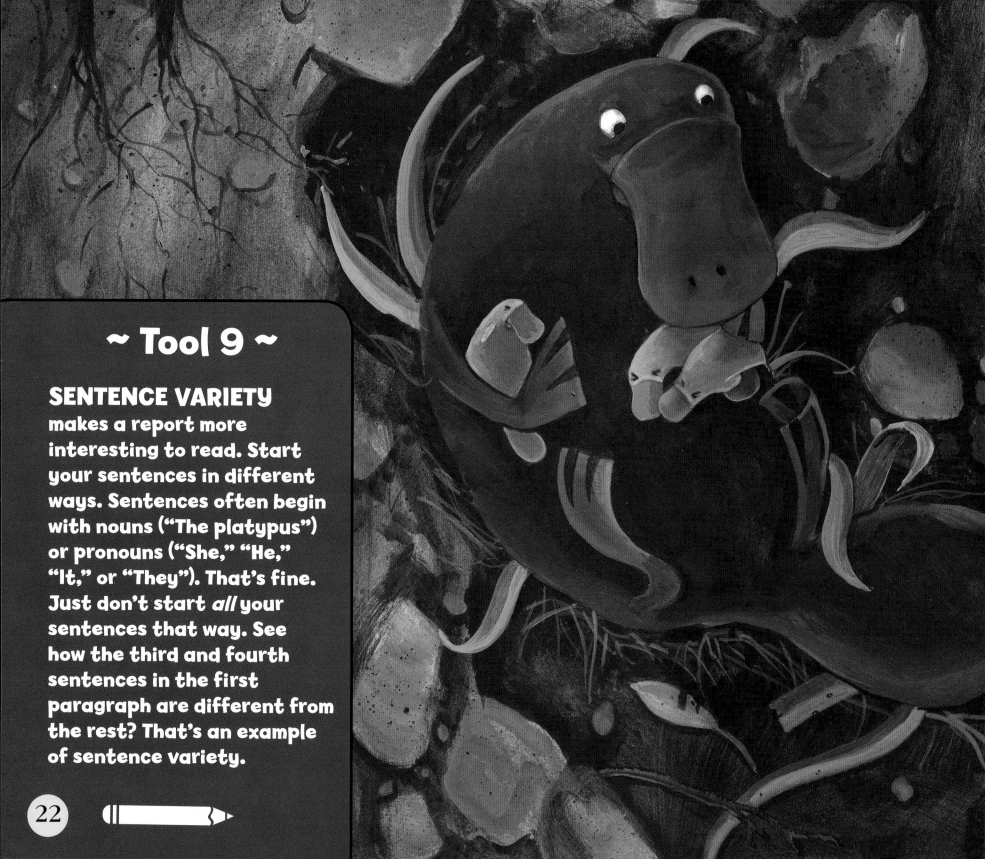

~ Tool 9 ~

SENTENCE VARIETY makes a report more interesting to read. Start your sentences in different ways. Sentences often begin with nouns ("The platypus") or pronouns ("She," "He," "It," or "They"). That's fine. Just don't start *all* your sentences that way. See how the third and fourth sentences in the first paragraph are different from the rest? That's an example of sentence variety.

This mammal has another very strange feature. It lays eggs! In spring, the female makes a long tunnel with a burrow at the end. Using her tail, she brings in leaves and reeds to line her burrow. She lays one to three small, leathery eggs. She keeps the eggs warm for about 10 days.

When the baby platypuses hatch, they are blind and hairless. They are called "puggles." They drink milk through tiny holes in the mother's skin. The puggles are fed by their mother for about four months. Then they leave the burrow and start learning how to catch their own food.

~ Tool 10 ~

The last paragraph in a research report is the **CONCLUSION**. Remind the reader of your main points. If possible, go back to an idea in your introduction. Bring your report to a pleasing close.

When the platypus was first seen by Europeans in 1798, people thought it was a prank. They couldn't believe that the creature was real. But now we know better. The platypus might look strange, but its bill helps it find and catch food. Its tail and webbed feet help it to swim and dig burrows. The platypus is no joke!

~ Tool 11 ~

REVISION is an important part of all good writing. Pretend you're reading your report for the very first time. Are your facts presented in an order that makes sense? Are you missing any important facts? Or have you included facts that aren't needed? You might need to cut, add, or move information.

~ Tool 12 ~

When you're happy with how your report is put together, it's time to **PROOFREAD.** Check your spelling. Make sure your commas, periods, and other punctuation are used correctly.

~ Tool 13 ~

The final step in writing a research report is a **BIBLIOGRAPHY.** A bibliography lets the reader know where you got your information. Bibliographies can be written in many different styles. Ask your teacher for help, or you can follow the example on page 27.

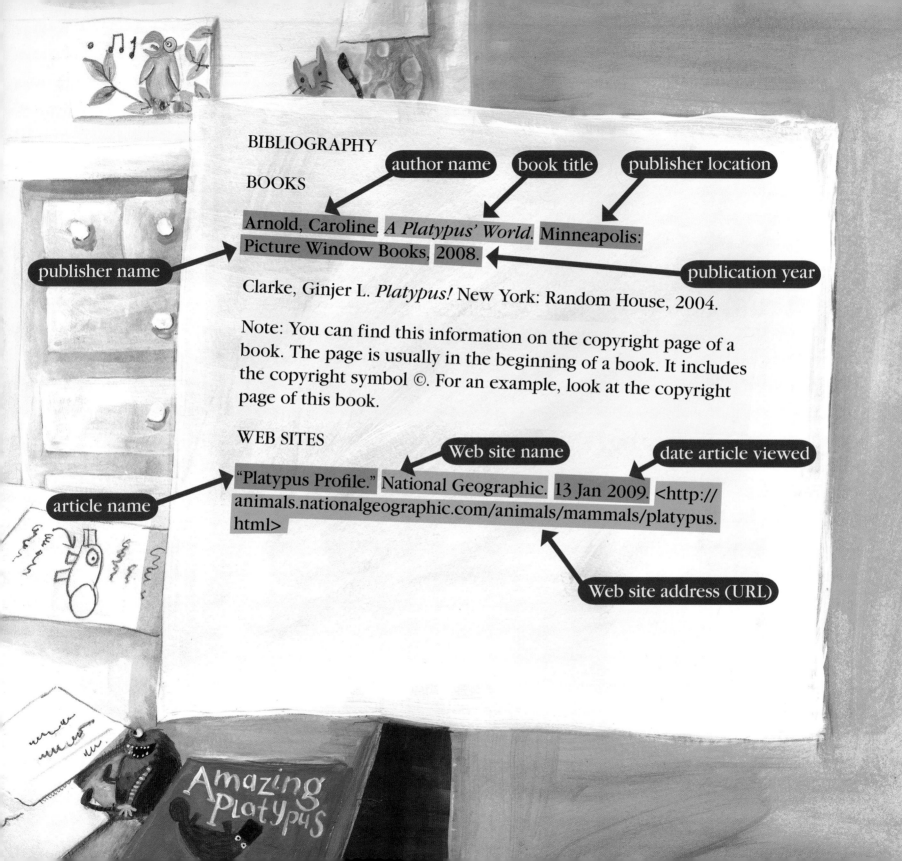

BIBLIOGRAPHY

author name   **book title**   **publisher location**

BOOKS

Arnold, Caroline. *A Platypus' World*. Minneapolis:
Picture Window Books, 2008.

publisher name   **publication year**

Clarke, Ginjer L. *Platypus!* New York: Random House, 2004.

Note: You can find this information on the copyright page of a
book. The page is usually in the beginning of a book. It includes
the copyright symbol ©. For an example, look at the copyright
page of this book.

WEB SITES

Web site name   **date article viewed**

"Platypus Profile." National Geographic. 13 Jan 2009. <http://
animals.nationalgeographic.com/animals/mammals/platypus.
html>

article name

Web site address (URL)

27

Let's Review!

These are the **13 tools** you need to write great research reports.

Every research report starts with a **TOPIC** **(1)**. Then the research begins. Good **SOURCES** **(2)** of information include books, magazines, and Web sites. **BRAINSTORMING** **(3)** helps the writer decide what information to include in the report. **NOTES** **(4)** and an **OUTLINE** **(5)** help organize the report and make writing easier.

The **INTRODUCTION** **(6)** lets readers know what the report is about. The **BODY** **(7)** contains most of the information. Every paragraph in the body should start with a **TOPIC SENTENCE** **(8)**. Starting sentences in different ways creates **SENTENCE VARIETY** **(9)** and makes the report more interesting to read. The last paragraph is the **CONCLUSION** **(10)**. It sums up the report and brings it to an end.

The **REVISION** **(11)** step allows the writer to add, cut, or move facts around. In the **PROOFREADING** **(12)** step, the writer takes a close look at spelling, punctuation, and grammar. The final part of the research report is the **BIBLIOGRAPHY** **(13)**. It lists the sources used to write the report.

Getting Started Exercises

- Writing a good research report takes time. To keep yourself on track, use a calendar. Give yourself deadlines for finding sources, writing an outline, finishing your first draft, and so on. That way, you can do your best work with every step. You won't feel rushed at the last minute.

- Are you having trouble picking a topic? Think about your favorite books, movies, and TV shows. Think about trips you've taken with your family. Ask people who their heroes are. If you do these things, you'll probably find a topic in no time. For example, maybe one of your favorite movies is about penguins. You could write a report on penguins, or about Antarctica. Or maybe your grandfather loves the music of Elvis Presley. Elvis would be a good topic.

- Chances are, your older siblings or friends have written research reports for school. Ask them if they have any advice. And if you run into trouble while you're writing your report, you can ask them for help, too.

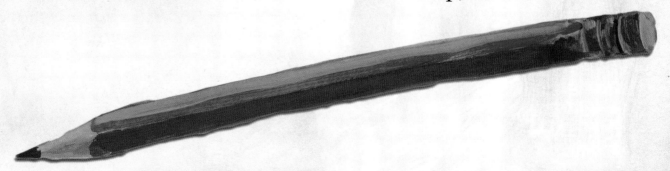

Writing Tips

When you take notes, don't copy from your sources word for word. Just write down a few key words. That way, when you start writing, you'll sound like yourself.

Sometimes the facts you find in one source will be different from the facts in another source. Ask your parents, teacher, or librarian which source is the best to use. If they don't know, go ahead and pick one source as your main one. Be consistent in using that source. For example, if you get an animal's weight from one source, get its length from that source, too.

Ask a friend, sibling, or parent to look over your report. They might see mistakes that you missed.

Put your finished report in a folder or sheet protector. That way, when you hand it in, it will be clean and unwrinkled.

Glossary

bibliography—a list of books, articles, and other sources that are used in the writing of a paper; the bibliography is placed at the end of the paper

body—the main part of a written piece

brainstorming—to come up with lots of ideas all at once, without stopping to judge them

conclusion—the final part of a written piece

consistent—to do something the same way every time

detail—a small part of a larger thing

expert—someone who knows a lot about a certain topic

index card—a small card made of heavy paper, used for taking notes

introduction—the first part of a written piece

notes—bits of written information

outline—the main points of a written piece, in the order they appear

research—to study a subject in an organized way

revision—changing a piece of writing to make it better

source—a book, article, person, or group that provides information about a topic

topic—a subject or main area of interest

topic sentence—the first sentence in a paragraph that tells what the paragraph will be about

variety—a group of things that are different from each other

To Learn More

More Books to Read

Kemper, David, Patrick Sebranek, and Verne Meyer. *Write Ahead: A Student Handbook for Writing and Learning*. Wilmington, Mass.: Write Source, 2004.

Madden, Kerry. *Writing Smarts: A Girl's Guide to Writing Great Poetry, Stories, School Reports, and More!* Middleton, Wis.: Pleasant Co., 2002.

Terban, Marvin. *Find It! Write It! Done! Your Fast and Fun Guide to Research Skills That Rock!* New York: Scholastic, 2007.

Internet Sites

FactHound offers a safe, fun way to find Internet sites related to this book. All of the sites on FactHound have been researched by our staff.

Here's all you do:
Visit *www.facthound.com*
FactHound will fetch the best sites for you!

Index

Look for all of the books in the Writer's Toolbox series:

It's All About You: Writing Your Own Journal
Just the Facts: Writing Your Own Research Report
Make Me Giggle: Writing Your Own Silly Story
Once Upon a Time: Writing Your Own Fairy Tale

Share a Scare: Writing Your Own Scary Story
Show Me a Story: Writing Your Own Picture Book
Sincerely Yours: Writing Your Own Letter
Words, Wit, and Wonder: Writing Your Own Poem